INSIDE THE NFL

TAMPA BAY BUCCANEERS

by Luke Hanlon

Abdo & Daughters
MIDDLE GRADE NONFICTION

An imprint of Abdo Publishing
abdobooks.com

Published by Abdo Publishing, a division of ABDO, PO Box 398166, Minneapolis, Minnesota 55439.

Printed in China.
052025
092025

THIS BOOK CONTAINS
RECYCLED MATERIALS

Cover Photos: Michael Hickey/Getty Images Sport/Getty Images (Mike Evans); Scott Halleran/Getty Images Sport/Getty Images (Derrick Brooks)
Interior Photos: Steve Luciano/AP Images, 4–5; Patrick Smith/Getty Images Sport/Getty Images, 6, 55, 63; Jim Rogash/Getty Images Sport/Getty Images, 7; Mike Ehrmann/Getty Images Sport/Getty Images, 8, 11, 59, 61 (top right), 61 (bottom left); Kevin C. Cox/Getty Images Sport/Getty Images, 9, 57, 61 (bottom right); Abdo Publishing, 12–13, 58; Focus on Sport/Getty Images Sport/Getty Images, 14–15, 22, 23; George Gojkovich/Getty Images Sport/Getty Images, 16, 26–27; Peter Read Miller/AP Images, 17, 60 (bottom left); AP Images, 18, 21; Focus on Sport/Getty Images, 19, 29, 30; James Drake/Sports Illustrated/Getty Images, 20; Sylvia Allen/Getty Images Sport/Getty Images, 24–25; Jay Dickman/Getty Images Sport/Getty Images, 28; Richard Drew/AP Images, 31; Scott Halleran/Getty Images Sport/Getty Images, 32; Chris O'Meara/AP Images, 33; Scott Audette/AP Images, 34; Steve Nesius/AP Images, 35, 47; Andy Lyons/Allsport/Getty Images Sport/Getty Images, 36–37; Joe Robbins/AP Images, 38–39, 60 (bottom right); David E. Klutho/Sports Illustrated/Getty Images, 40; Al Bello/Allsport/Getty Images Sport/Getty Images, 41; Al Messerschmidt/Getty Images Sport/Getty Images, 43, 50; Greg Trott/AP Images, 44, 54; Chris Gardner/AP Images, 45; Doug Pensinger/Getty Images Sport/Getty Images, 46, 48–49, 60 (top); J. Meric/Getty Images Sport/Getty Images, 51; Katharine Lotze/Getty Images Sport/Getty Images, 52, 61 (top left); Perry Knotts/AP Images, 53

Editor: Chrös McDougall
Series Designer: Laura Graphenteen
Production Designer: Ebonee Estrella

Library of Congress Control Number: 2024948479

Publisher's Cataloging-in-Publication Data

Names: Hanlon, Luke, author.
Title: Tampa Bay Buccaneers / by Luke Hanlon
Description: Minneapolis, Minnesota: Abdo Publishing, 2026 | Series: Inside the NFL | Includes online resources and index.
Identifiers: ISBN 9781098296919 (lib. bdg.) | ISBN 9798384919438 (ebook)
Subjects: LCSH: Tampa Bay Buccaneers (Football team)--Juvenile literature. | National Football League--Juvenile literature. | Football teams--Juvenile literature. | American football--Juvenile literature.
Classification: DDC 796.333--dc23

CONTENTS

Super Bowl LV in February 2021 was Tom Brady's 10th championship game and his first with the Tampa Bay Buccaneers.

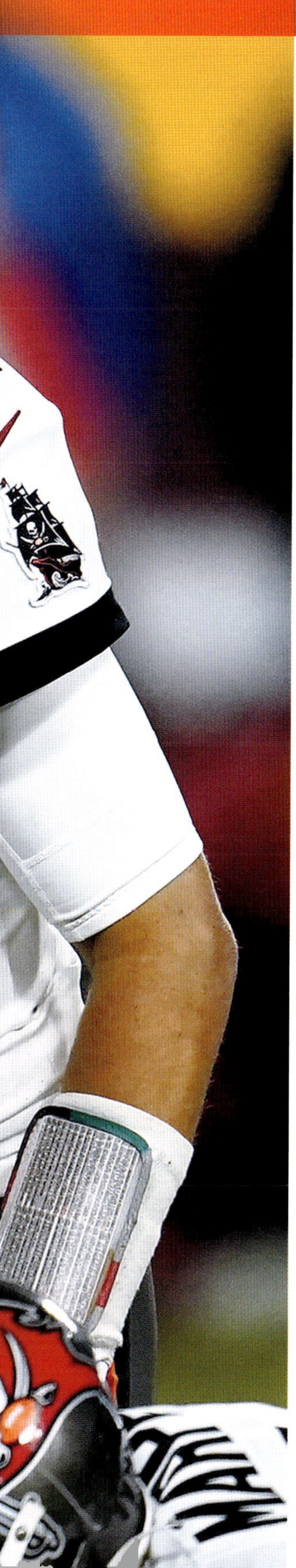

CHAPTER 1

LEGENDARY CONNECTION

Tampa Bay Buccaneers quarterback Tom Brady faked a handoff, drawing the Kansas City Chiefs' defense to running back Leonard Fournette. Then Brady turned and tossed a short pass to Rob Gronkowski. The big tight end caught it in stride behind the line of scrimmage. The fake handoff bought "Gronk" just enough time to slip untouched into the end zone.

The score put the Buccaneers up 7–3 near the end of the first quarter in Super Bowl LV on February 7, 2021. The play also marked the 13th time Brady had thrown a touchdown pass to Gronkowski in the playoffs. No duo had connected for more scores in National Football League (NFL) postseason history. However, most of those touchdowns came when the legendary duo played for a different team.

SETTING THE STANDARD

Brady played the first 20 years of his NFL career with the New England Patriots. He had already won three Super Bowls by the time Gronkowski arrived in 2010. The 6-foot-6-inch, 265-pound tight end quickly became Brady's favorite target.

Buccaneers tight end Rob Gronkowski spikes the ball after scoring a touchdown during Super Bowl LV.

With Brady's accurate passes and Gronkowski's athleticism, the duo tore up opposing defenses. And both players seemed to elevate their games once the playoffs started. They helped New England reach five more Super Bowls and win three between the 2011 and 2018 seasons. The run of dominance established Brady as the most successful quarterback in league history. Gronkowski, meanwhile, showed just how dominant a big, athletic, pass-catching tight end could be. The only things that seemed to slow him were frequent injuries. He retired after winning his third Super Bowl following the 2018 season. Brady played one more season in New England in 2019. Then, at age 42, he decided he wanted to try something new.

MOVING SOUTH

As a free agent, Brady was able to sign with any team in 2020. And just about every team wanted him. Soon after Brady joined the Buccaneers on a two-year deal, Gronkowski announced he was coming out of retirement to join his old teammate in Tampa Bay.

The Buccaneers had a spotty history as a franchise. They'd done more losing than winning since their 1976 debut. And the former Patriots were coming to a team that had missed the playoffs for 12 seasons in a row. But Brady and Gronkowski saw great potential

Brady, *right*, and Gronkowski connected for 90 touchdowns while with the New England Patriots. Only two other quarterback-receiver duos in NFL history had more.

Brady threw for seven touchdowns in three playoff games to lead the Bucs to Super Bowl LV.

in the young squad. They thought they could elevate the Bucs to new heights. That plan appeared to be working when Tampa Bay won 11 games and returned to the playoffs in 2020. Brady and Gronkowski connected for seven touchdowns along the way.

The National Football Conference (NFC) had lots of good teams, though. Tampa Bay would have to beat three of them to reach the Super Bowl, and all three games would be on the road. Gronkowski didn't have a catch as the Bucs held off the Washington Football Team in the playoff opener. He had a single catch against the New Orleans Saints in the next round, but the Bucs won again. Then they went to Green Bay and beat the Packers in the NFC Championship Game. That clinched the team's second trip to the Super Bowl.

Tampa Bay faced the defending champion Chiefs in Super Bowl LV. Brady's first-quarter touchdown pass to Gronkowski got the Buccaneers on the board. They led 7–3 midway through the second quarter when they lined up on first-and-10. This time Brady faked a handoff to Fournette and dropped back to pass. His offensive line shoved the Chiefs back to give Brady time. Finally, the quarterback spotted Gronkowski, who had slipped into space. Brady rifled a pass to the back of the end zone. It went right to Gronkowski's hands for a 17-yard score, putting Tampa Bay up 14–3.

HOME SWEET HOME

Well before the 2020 season, the NFL had selected Tampa Bay's Raymond James Stadium to host Super Bowl LV. When the Buccaneers reached the game, they became the first team in 55 Super Bowls to play it in their home stadium. The stadium wasn't as full as it usually is, though. Because of the COVID-19 pandemic, the NFL allowed only 24,835 fans to attend. Raymond James Stadium can hold up to 75,000.

Gronkowski hauls in one of his six catches during Super Bowl LV.

No lead was safe against the Chiefs, though. Behind hotshot young quarterback Patrick Mahomes, Kansas City could carve up opposing defenses with ease. And the Chiefs got three points back on a field goal on their next possession. Their only mistake was scoring with 1:01 left before halftime.

With an opportunity to destroy the Chiefs' hopes of a comeback, Brady quickly got to work from the Bucs' 35-yard line. Soon facing a critical third down, he hit Gronkowski for a 5-yard gain to move the chains. Three plays later, the Bucs reached Kansas City's 1-yard line. With 10 seconds remaining before halftime, Brady calmly faked a handoff. Then he delivered a precise pass to wide receiver Antonio Brown in the end zone. Instead of leading by eight points, the Bucs went to the locker room up 21–6.

Kansas City would need a huge second half to stay in the game. A field goal on the opening drive created some hope for Chiefs fans. Then Brady crushed their dreams once and for all. On the Buccaneers' first drive of the second half, Brady connected with Gronkowski over the middle of the field for a 25-yard gain. That set up a touchdown run by Fournette, and Tampa Bay cruised from there to win 31–9.

Brady earned the Super Bowl Most Valuable Player (MVP) Award for his performance. But he couldn't have won it without his good buddy Gronk, who finished the game with 67 yards and two touchdowns. The uniforms had changed, but Brady and Gronkowski showed they were still the NFL's most feared combination. And for fans in Tampa Bay, the two superstars delivered a season they would never forget.

Brady, *right*, celebrates with Gronkowski after the Buccaneers won Super Bowl LV.

NFL TEAMS MAP

NFC EAST

- DALLAS COWBOYS
- NEW YORK GIANTS
- PHILADELPHIA EAGLES
- WASHINGTON COMMANDERS

NFC WEST

- ARIZONA CARDINALS
- LOS ANGELES RAMS
- SAN FRANCISCO 49ERS
- SEATTLE SEAHAWKS

NFC NORTH

- CHICAGO BEARS
- DETROIT LIONS
- GREEN BAY PACKERS
- MINNESOTA VIKINGS

NFC SOUTH

- ATLANTA FALCONS
- CAROLINA PANTHERS
- NEW ORLEANS SAINTS
- TAMPA BAY BUCCANEERS

AFC

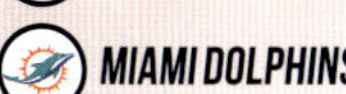

AFC EAST

- BUFFALO BILLS
- MIAMI DOLPHINS
- NEW ENGLAND PATRIOTS
- NEW YORK JETS

AFC WEST

- DENVER BRONCOS
- KANSAS CITY CHIEFS
- LAS VEGAS RAIDERS
- LOS ANGELES CHARGERS

AFC NORTH

- BALTIMORE RAVENS
- CINCINNATI BENGALS
- CLEVELAND BROWNS
- PITTSBURGH STEELERS

AFC SOUTH

- HOUSTON TEXANS
- INDIANAPOLIS COLTS
- JACKSONVILLE JAGUARS
- TENNESSEE TITANS

Buccaneers quarterback Steve Spurrier drops back to pass during the team's first season in 1976.

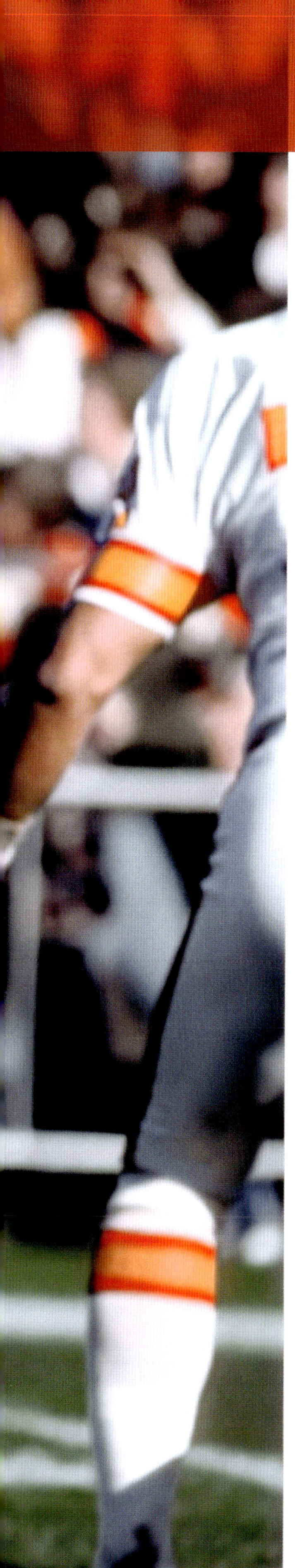

CHAPTER 2

ROUGH START

THE NFL WENT INTO THE 1970s LOOKING TO GROW BEYOND ITS 26 teams. In 1974, the league took the next step by awarding expansion teams to Tampa Bay and Seattle. The new teams would begin playing in 1976.

One of the first orders of business for Tampa Bay owner Hugh Culverhouse was picking a name for the team. Fans submitted roughly 400 ideas to a name-the-team contest. Culverhouse chose the Buccaneers, named for the pirates who visited western Florida during the 1600s.

The Buccaneers would play home games at Tampa Stadium, a relatively new facility that added thousands of additional seats in preparation for the NFL. For the team's first head coach, Culverhouse made a bold move. John McKay had won four college national championships over 16 seasons leading the University of Southern California (USC) Trojans. However, the Buccaneers' job was his first coaching professional football. And he would have to work with a group of largely inexperienced players.

Going into the 1976 season, each existing NFL team got to protect 29 of its players. The Bucs and Seahawks then got to select from the unprotected players in an expansion draft. This meant the new teams were getting mostly backup players or players the existing teams didn't want. The Bucs had brighter prospects in the 1976 NFL Draft. With the first overall pick, they selected Lee Roy Selmon. The 6-foot-3-inch, 256-pound defensive lineman had been a college star at Oklahoma. Tampa Bay fans hoped his game-wrecking skills would carry over to the NFL.

John McKay arrived in Tampa with a reputation as a great college coach at USC.

Defensive lineman Lee Roy Selmon went on to make six Pro Bowls during his nine seasons with the Buccaneers.

NO WINS IN SIGHT

Expansion teams, with their lack of talent, often struggle in their first seasons. McKay was fully aware of this. Ahead of the season, he tried to lighten the mood in the locker room and joke with his players. Before the Buccaneers even played a game, McKay told his team, "It bothers me that they [the national media] have picked us to be the worst team in football. Because what they are doing now is challenging your physical and your mental capacity and my ability to coach you. Now, this hurts me. Second-worst team, I could stand it. But not the worst team."

That humor didn't lead to success on the field. In their first two games, the Bucs didn't score a single point. Things looked better in Week 3 when they jumped out to a 6–0 lead against the Buffalo Bills. Then kicker Dave Green drilled his third field goal of the game to put the Bucs ahead 9–7 in the fourth quarter. However, the Bills scored a late touchdown to win 14–9.

Spurrier was sacked 32 times during the 1976 season.

Losses continued to pile up. Some of the few bright spots that season came from Selmon, who racked up five sacks through his first eight games. But multiple injuries forced him to miss the final six games of the season. Without Selmon, an already horrible Tampa Bay defense got even worse. The Buccaneers finished the season 0–14, making them the first NFL team in the Super Bowl era to lose all its games in a single season.

Despite the many blowout losses, McKay never lost his sense of humor. Throughout the 1976 season, he joked with the media about how bad the Buccaneers were. After one loss, McKay said, "We didn't tackle well today, but we made up for it by not blocking."

> **"WE DIDN'T TACKLE WELL TODAY, BUT WE MADE UP FOR IT BY NOT BLOCKING."**
>
> **—JOHN MCKAY**

ENDING THE STREAK

Tampa Bay's winless season did come with the benefit of receiving the top pick in the 1977 draft. The Buccaneers used that pick on Ricky Bell, a talented running back McKay had coached at USC. However, Bell was unable to re-create his college success as a rookie as Tampa Bay once again struggled to score.

McKay, *right*, became known for his sense of humor, even as the losses piled up for Tampa Bay.

Behind a healthy Selmon in 1977, the Buccaneers' defense kept the team in games. But that didn't translate to wins. With an 0-12 record, the Bucs appeared to be headed toward another winless season. They traveled to New Orleans for a late-season game against the Saints. At 3-9, the Saints were hardly a powerhouse. Yet, Saints quarterback

Bucs running back Ricky Bell (42) ran for 436 yards as a rookie in 1977.

Archie Manning said it would be a disgrace to lose to the Buccaneers. Tampa Bay's defense made Manning regret those words.

The Buccaneers intercepted Manning three times. Eventually, Saints head coach Hank Stram benched Manning for backup Bobby Scott. He didn't fare any better. The Bucs picked him off three times as well. That dominant performance led Tampa Bay to a 33–14 win. And with it, the Bucs' 26-game losing streak was over.

Linebacker Richard Wood, *holding helmet*, and the Bucs celebrate after beating the New Orleans Saints in 1977.

The Bucs carried that momentum into the final week of the season. This time, they forced the St. Louis Cardinals into four turnovers on the way to a 17–7 win at Tampa Stadium. The fans, so excited to finally see a win in their home stadium, celebrated by tearing down the goalposts after the game.

CREAMSICLE JERSEYS

The Buccaneers came into the NFL with a unique look. The team's pastel orange jerseys featured white numbers outlined in red. Fans nicknamed them "Creamsicle" jerseys after the orange frozen treat. The Bucs wore these jerseys until they changed their logo and colors in 1997. The team brought back the Creamsicle jerseys for one game each season from 2009 to 2012. The Bucs restarted that tradition in 2023.

SURPRISE RUN

For the third year in a row, Tampa Bay headed into the NFL Draft with the top pick. But McKay, knowing his roster had many holes to fill, traded the pick to the Houston Oilers. In return, the Bucs got four draft picks and tight end Jimmie Giles. Now picking 17th, the Bucs selected quarterback Doug Williams, making him the first Black quarterback ever taken in the first round of the draft.

After Williams started 10 games in another losing season in 1978, he got the Bucs off to a good start in 1979. In Week 1, he connected with Giles for a 66-yard touchdown as Tampa Bay easily beat the Detroit Lions. Behind Williams, Bell, and Giles, the Buccaneers finally had a decent offense. Meanwhile, the defense continued to be strong as it allowed the fewest points in the NFL that season. After starting the season 9–3, the Bucs needed just one more win to clinch their division crown and a spot in the playoffs for the first time.

Tight end Jimmie Giles made four Pro Bowls while playing with the Buccaneers.

Quarterback Doug Williams threw for 73 touchdowns in 67 career games for the Bucs.

The last win proved tough to come by. First the Minnesota Vikings blocked four Bucs field-goal attempts to defeat Tampa Bay 23–22. The Chicago Bears shut out the Buccaneers the next week. Then the Bucs traveled to San Francisco only to turn the ball over six times in an ugly loss to the lowly 49ers. That set up an all-or-nothing Week 16 matchup against the Kansas City Chiefs.

Rain poured down in Tampa Bay throughout the game, making it difficult for either team to pass. Instead, Bell gashed Kansas City for 147 rushing yards. Turning those yards into points proved to be

a challenge, though, and the teams went into the fourth quarter tied 0–0. Finally, Bucs kicker Neil O'Donoghue drilled a 19-yard field goal to secure a 3–0 win. After a brutal start for the franchise, the Buccaneers became the fastest expansion team to win its division. More importantly, they were headed to the playoffs.

Playing at home in the divisional round, Bell ran for a pair of touchdowns to help the Bucs go up 17–0 on the Philadelphia Eagles. Williams later connected with Giles for another touchdown to

Bell (42) ran for 142 yards in the playoff game against the Philadelphia Eagles in December 1979.

help secure a 24–17 win. In only their fourth season, the Bucs were headed to the NFC Championship Game.

Playing at home again, the Buccaneers were stout on defense. They limited the Los Angeles Rams to three field goals. However, Williams struggled early, completing only two of 13 pass attempts. McKay benched Williams for backup Mike Rae, but he also completed only two passes. The Bucs' dream season ended with a 9–0 shutout loss to the Rams.

Doug Williams gave the Buccaneers stability at the quarterback position.

CHAPTER 3

TRY AND TRY AGAIN

BUILDING ON THE MAGICAL 1979 PLAYOFF RUN PROVED DIFFICULT FOR the Buccaneers. Throughout the 1980 season, they frequently fell behind early and then relied on Doug Williams to bring them back. While the quarterback was able to lead a league-high five fourth-quarter comebacks, it still wasn't enough to lift the Bucs to a winning record.

Such late drama became routine for Tampa Bay in the early 1980s. In 1981, the Bucs' playoff hopes came down to the final game. Traveling to Detroit, where the Lions hadn't lost at home all season, Tampa Bay took a 10-point lead in the fourth quarter. Then the Bucs held on for a 20–17 win and the division title. Their postseason run didn't last long, however, as Williams threw four interceptions in a 38–0 demolition by the Dallas Cowboys.

After the Buccaneers started the 1982 season 0–2, the NFL shut down due to a players' strike. When the league resumed two months later, teams played an additional seven regular-season games. The Bucs rolled to five wins, all of them coming by six points or fewer. Williams led Tampa Bay back from 15- and 17-point deficits to win its final two games. But the magic ran out in the playoffs. Though the Bucs led the Cowboys entering the fourth quarter, a pick six by Williams began a 14-point Cowboys run as they went on to win 30–17.

DRAFT DAY DISASTER

The Buccaneers' front office decided to stay in Tampa Bay during the 1982 draft. When it was time to pick, they'd pass their choice on to the team's equipment manager Pat Marcuccillo, who was at the draft in New York City. With the 17th pick, the Bucs considered offensive lineman Sean Farrell and defensive lineman Booker Reese. Ultimately, team officials told Marcuccillo they weren't taking Farrell and wanted Reese. But Marcuccillo heard only Farrell's name, so that's who he submitted to the league. In a panic move, the Bucs then traded their 1983 first-round pick to move back up in the 1982 draft and take Reese.

FALLING APART

Though Tampa Bay's playoff struggles frustrated fans, the team had come a long way since its early days as a laughingstock. Having a reliable quarterback in Williams played a big role in that. However, despite leading the team to three

Bucs running back Melvin Carter tries to outrun a Dallas Cowboys defender during a January 1983 playoff game.

John McKay coached the Bucs to a 44-88-1 record over nine seasons.

playoff appearances in four years, he was the lowest-paid starting quarterback in the league. Even multiple backups made more.

So when Williams's contract expired after the 1982 season, he asked the Bucs for a fair salary. Instead, owner Hugh Culverhouse refused to meet the player's demands. When the two couldn't come to an agreement, Williams opted to leave for the rival United States Football League (USFL). It was the first of several personnel decisions the Bucs would come to regret in the coming years.

Without Williams, the consistency the Buccaneers had built up came tumbling down. Over the next two seasons, the team won eight total games. Following the 1984 season, head coach John McKay resigned due to health concerns. That year also proved to be the end of Lee Roy Selmon's career, as he suffered a severe back injury. As for Williams, he returned to the NFL in 1986, this time with Washington. One year later, he led the team to a Super Bowl title.

MISSING OUT

One way the USFL tried to establish itself was by offering top college players a lot of money to forgo the NFL and join the new league instead. That was the case with Steve Young, the former Brigham Young University star quarterback who became the first pick in the 1984 USFL draft. In case players such as Young ever changed their minds, the NFL held a supplemental draft so its teams could also claim the rights to those players.

So the Bucs took a chance on Young and picked him first overall in the 1984 supplemental draft. That decision paid off when Young left the floundering USFL in 1985 and joined up with Tampa Bay. The athletic lefty showed all the physical traits teams would want in a quarterback. However, he joined a Bucs team without much talent to work with. Young often had to run for his life due to poor blocking. And if he did have time to throw, his receivers usually struggled to get open.

The Bucs had a chance to get Young some much-needed help in the 1986 draft. Following a 2–14 season, they held the top draft pick. Almost everyone agreed they should take Bo Jackson. The former Auburn running back had won the Heisman Trophy as college football's best player in 1985. On top of his running skills, the ultra-athletic Jackson also

Steve Young showed promise as a dual-threat quarterback over his 19 games with Tampa Bay.

Highly touted Auburn running back Bo Jackson, *right*, poses with NFL commissioner Pete Rozelle at the 1986 draft.

played baseball at Auburn and had Major League Baseball teams interested in him.

Before the draft, Culverhouse flew Jackson to Tampa Bay on his private plane for a meeting. Though Culverhouse had assured Jackson this was OK, accepting a free flight was against college rules. As a result, Jackson could no longer play baseball at Auburn. Furious with Culverhouse for ending his college baseball career, Jackson said he'd never play for the owner. Culverhouse picked the star running back anyway, and then he offered the player a lot more money than if he'd sign with baseball's Kansas City Royals. But Jackson stayed true to his word and went to play baseball instead.

Meanwhile, Young played through another miserable season in 1986. In 19 career starts with Tampa Bay, he won only three games. The Bucs decided it was time for a change. Ahead of the 1987 season, they traded Young to the San Francisco 49ers.

Jackson ended up joining the NFL in 1987, but as a member of the Los Angeles Raiders. He showed flashes of brilliance with the Raiders and made the 1990 Pro Bowl before injuries cut his career short. Young, on the other hand, went on to have a Hall of Fame career and led the 49ers to a Super Bowl title. As with Williams, Tampa Bay fans could only watch and wonder, "What if?"

NEW IDENTITY

The Buccaneers remained one of the NFL's worst teams for years. Under the penny-pinching Culverhouse, the Bucs consistently had one of the NFL's lowest payrolls. In 1991, Culverhouse died at the age of 75. That year, the Buccaneers completed their ninth straight season with at least 10 losses. They went on to add three more to that dubious streak.

Over their first 19 seasons, the Bucs had posted 16 losing seasons and made the playoffs just three times. Some wondered if pro football had a future in Tampa Bay. In January 1995, the team got new life when Malcolm Glazer bought it. The businessman,

Linebacker Hardy Nickerson racked up a Buccaneers-record 214 tackles in 1993.

Safety John Lynch (47) recorded more than 100 tackles in three different seasons with the Bucs.

originally from upstate New York, vowed to spend what it took to make the team better while keeping it in Tampa Bay.

Glazer came into a team that had already acquired some talented players. Hardy Nickerson, a physical linebacker, signed with the Bucs in 1993. Tampa Bay drafted hard-hitting safety John Lynch the same year. With two first-round draft picks in 1995, the Buccaneers brought in defensive tackle Warren Sapp and linebacker Derrick Brooks, who both went on to Hall of Fame careers. The next step was finding the right coach to put everything together.

A few years earlier, the Bucs had interviewed a promising young assistant named Tony Dungy before hiring Sam Wyche as their head coach. After a fourth consecutive losing season under Wyche in 1995, the team fired him. By then, Dungy had become a respected defensive coordinator with the Minnesota Vikings. This time, the Bucs decided he was the right man for the job.

Dungy brought a new style of defense to the Buccaneers. Many teams had run a "Cover 2" scheme in which the two safeties each cover half the field. Dungy tweaked that classic defense to have the middle linebacker drop deeper into coverage. This scheme became known as the "Tampa 2" defense.

While the Bucs' offense struggled mightily in Dungy's first year, the defense was dominant with Nickerson playing the vital middle linebacker role. In 1997, the Bucs combined that stingy defense with a newly effective rushing attack to go 10–6. It was the team's first winning record since 1982.

The dynamic "Thunder and Lightning" backfield duo of fullback Mike Alstott and rookie running back Warrick Dunn played a big

Tony Dungy arrived in Tampa with a reputation for coaching great defenses.

Tampa Bay defenders swarm the Detroit Lions punter during their playoff game after the 1997 season.

role in the team's success. Alstott used his 248-pound frame to barrel over helpless defenders, while Dunn evaded tacklers with his speed and agility. Meanwhile, Tampa Bay's defense ranked among the top three in fewest points and yards allowed.

In the playoffs, the Bucs leaned on their strengths. Dunn and Alstott combined to run for 140 yards, while the defense shut down the Detroit Lions to secure a 20–10 win. It was the team's first playoff win in 18 years. Though the Bucs lost in the next round, it was clear that Dungy had the team moving in the right direction.

Defensive tackle Warren Sapp recorded 77 sacks during his career with the Buccaneers.

CHAPTER 4

CLIMBING THE MOUNTAIN

UNDER TONY DUNGY, THE BUCCANEERS CONSISTENTLY BOASTED ONE OF the league's best defenses. Tampa Bay allowed fewer than 15 points per game in 1999. Warren Sapp was the unit's anchor. He racked up 12 1/2 sacks and won the Defensive Player of the Year Award. Defensive teammates Derrick Brooks, John Lynch, and Hardy Nickerson joined Sapp on the Pro Bowl roster.

The team's elite defense led the Bucs to their first division title since 1979. And the defense continued to shine in the playoffs. Although Washington jumped to a 13–0 lead in the divisional round, thanks in part to a kick return touchdown, the Bucs' defense held firm from there. Running back Mike Alstott and tight end John Davis each ran for touchdowns as Tampa Bay came back to win 14–13.

For as stout as the Bucs' defense had been all year, the St. Louis Rams were electric on offense. The Rams not only had the league's best offense, but they also had one of the highest-scoring offenses in NFL history, which was led by MVP quarterback Kurt Warner. When the two high-powered units met in the NFC title game for a chance to move on to the Super Bowl, St. Louis was favored to win by two touchdowns.

Bucs linebacker Derrick Brooks drags down St. Louis Rams wide receiver Issac Bruce during the NFC title game in January 2000.

The underdog Bucs quickly showed they were up for the challenge. On the first play of the game, Tampa Bay defensive lineman Steve White deflected and then picked off a pass by Warner. That was a sign of things to come. After throwing just 13 interceptions all season, Warner threw three to the Bucs in this game alone. However, Tampa Bay's offense struggled to take advantage of the turnovers.

Buccaneers wide receiver Bert Emanuel holds on to the ball while hitting the ground during the NFC Championship Game.

Trailing 6–5, the Rams got the ball back with just over eight minutes to play. Seven plays later, Warner connected with wide receiver Ricky Proehl for a 30-yard touchdown, putting St. Louis up 11–6 with 4:44 on the clock. Tampa Bay's defense had played a nearly flawless game until that point. Now the fate of the team's season came down to the offense.

Rookie quarterback Shaun King began leading the Bucs up the field. After nine plays, they faced a second-and-23 from the Rams' 35-yard line. On the next play, King fired a 12-yard pass that wide receiver Bert Emanuel dived to catch. However, the officials reviewed the play and ruled it an incomplete pass because the tip of the ball had touched the ground. The Rams then stopped the next two plays and secured the trip to the Super Bowl.

The no-catch call caused immediate controversy. The NFL has since clarified its criteria for a catch. Now, as long as the receiver maintains control of the ball when it hits the ground, as Emanuel did, the catch stands. That change became known as "the Bert Emanuel Rule." However, it didn't help the 1999 Buccaneers.

SAME ISSUES

Behind another stellar defense, the Bucs won 10 games in 2000. However, they again fell apart in the playoffs. Tampa Bay failed to score a touchdown in a blowout loss at the Philadelphia Eagles in the wild-card round.

For Bucs fans, a trend was emerging. Each season, Dungy was able to put together a powerful defense. However, the team could go only so far without more effective play on offense. Inconsistency at the quarterback position had been a particular issue. So before

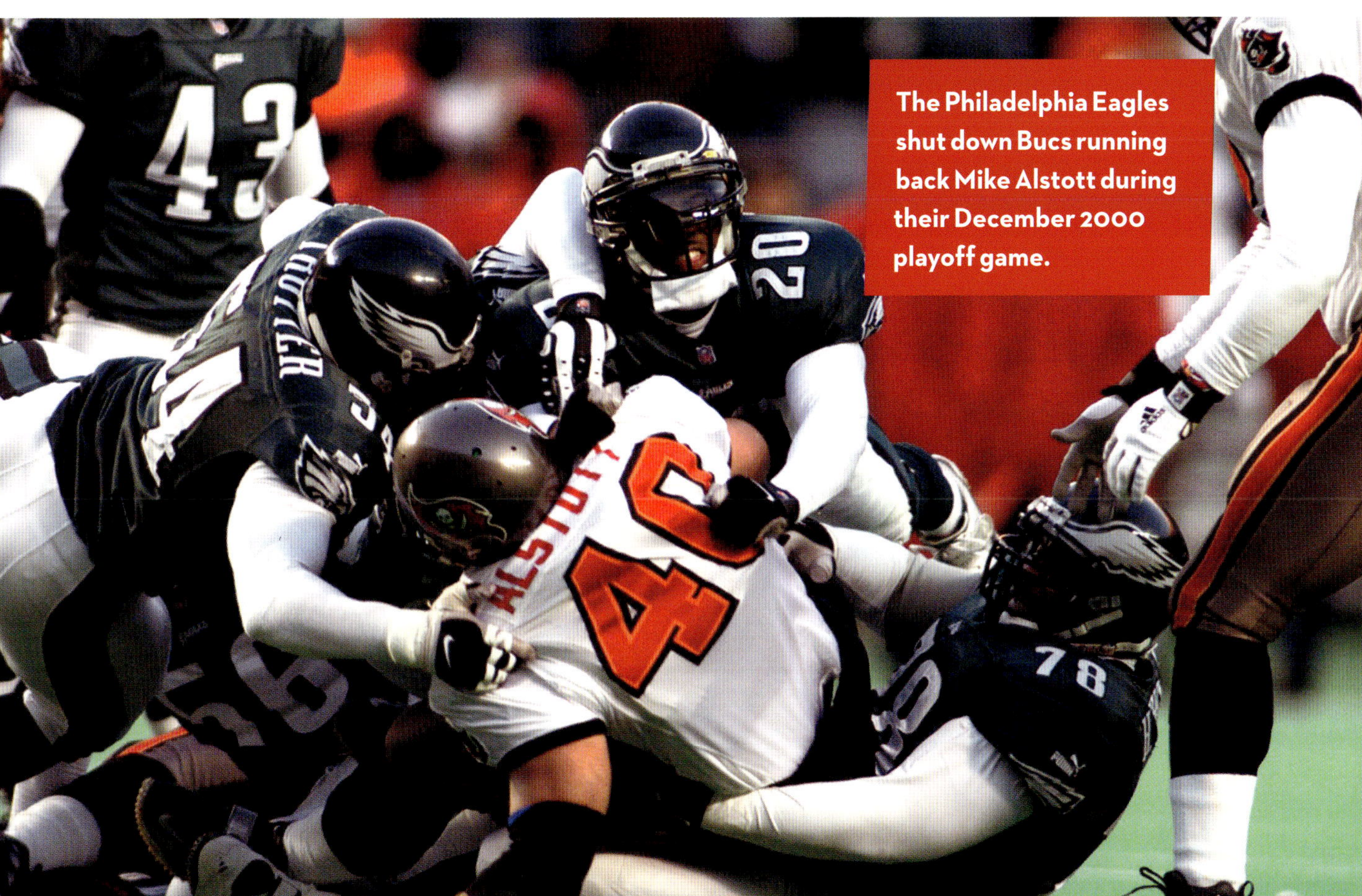

The Philadelphia Eagles shut down Bucs running back Mike Alstott during their December 2000 playoff game.

the 2001 season, Tampa Bay looked to solve that problem by signing former Pro Bowl pick Brad Johnson. The team also brought in star defensive end Simeon Rice to bolster an already elite unit. Those moves made it clear that the Bucs intended to make a Super Bowl run in 2001.

The Bucs didn't look much like a Super Bowl contender during the regular season, finishing just 9–7. But that record was still good enough to make the playoffs. Once again, they opened on the road in Philadelphia. And once again, the Bucs' offense failed to get into the end zone in a 31–9 defeat. After another quick postseason exit, the Buccaneers fired Dungy.

FIRE THE CANNONS

The Buccaneers built Raymond James Stadium ahead of the 1998 season. Wanting to make it specific to the team, the Bucs added one of the more unique features in any NFL stadium. Behind one of the end zones is a 103-foot (31 m) pirate ship. The ship features cannons that shoot off every time the Buccaneers score. Six shots fire after the Bucs score a touchdown. Then a seventh is fired if the team converts the extra point.

BLOCKBUSTER DEAL

Members of the press reported that the team wanted Bill Parcells to take over as head coach. He had established himself as an all-time great while leading the New York Giants to a pair of Super Bowl wins. But Parcells had retired from coaching in 1999. Despite the interest from the Bucs, Parcells decided to stay retired.

The team interviewed other top candidates as well, but Bucs officials couldn't agree on whom to hire. Owner Malcolm Glazer remained confident the team's defense could still be successful, so he desperately searched for an offensive coach. Finally, Glazer

Bucs defensive end Simeon Rice recorded 11 sacks during the 2001 season.

identified his target: Jon Gruden. There was just one problem. Gruden was coaching the Oakland Raiders.

The Raiders weren't looking to get rid of Gruden. He had just led the team to the American Football Conference (AFC) Championship Game and still had a year remaining on his contract. Nonetheless, Glazer called Raiders owner Al Davis to see what they could work out. Ultimately, the Bucs agreed to send four high draft picks and $8 million to the Raiders in exchange for Gruden. It was a steep price to pay, but Glazer was willing to shell out for the coach he thought could lift the Bucs to the Super Bowl.

Brooks led the league in tackles three times during his career.

CHALLENGE ACCEPTED

Gruden didn't want to tinker much with the Bucs' defense. He elected to keep Monte Kiffin as defensive coordinator, a role Kiffin had held since 1996. But Gruden sent a message to his new defense during training camp. He wanted the unit to be even more dominant in 2002. Specifically, he challenged the defense to score nine touchdowns.

Derrick Brooks took Gruden's challenge head-on. During the regular season, the instinctive linebacker scored four times on the way to winning the NFL's Defensive Player of the Year Award. Though the Bucs added only one other defensive touchdown, the defense was otherwise exceptional while allowing the fewest points and yards in the league. Meanwhile, Johnson's steady play at quarterback kept the offense moving. The Bucs won a team-record 12 games and cruised to a division title.

In the playoffs, Tampa Bay held the San Francisco 49ers without a touchdown in a divisional-round blowout. Then Bucs star cornerback Ronde Barber sealed a 27–10 win over the Eagles with a 92-yard pick six in the NFC title game. On the strength of Tampa Bay's sixth defensive touchdown, the team was headed to its first Super Bowl. In a twist of fate, the Bucs were set to meet the Raiders for the league championship.

Cornerback Ronde Barber runs an interception for a touchdown to clinch the Bucs win in the NFC Championship Game on January 19, 2003.

Gruden said he felt weird about facing his old team. The Raiders didn't like it either. "My immediate, instantaneous thought was that this would be a problem," Raiders CEO Amy Trask said, "as Jon knew our personnel inside out."

"MY IMMEDIATE, INSTANTANEOUS THOUGHT WAS THAT THIS WOULD BE A PROBLEM, AS JON [GRUDEN] KNEW OUR PERSONNEL INSIDE OUT."

—OAKLAND RAIDERS CEO AMY TRASK

That started with Rich Gannon. Gruden had helped the quarterback turn his career around in Oakland. Gannon kept that success going in 2002, earning league MVP honors while guiding an explosive Raiders offense. Against his former coach in the Super Bowl, though, Gannon looked like a backup. The Bucs constantly pressured him and shut down Oakland's offense.

Midway through the third quarter, Johnson and wide receiver Keenan McCardell connected for their second touchdown of the game to give the Bucs a 27–3 lead. The game was all but over. But the Bucs' defense, still thinking of Gruden's challenge in training

Tampa Bay wide receiver Keenan McCardell scored two touchdowns in Super Bowl XXXVII on January 26, 2003.

camp, kept up the intensity. In the third quarter, cornerback Dwight Smith picked off Gannon and took it to the end zone. Then Brooks added a pick six of his own with 1:18 left in the game. And the defense still wouldn't let up. With the clock winding down, Smith hauled in a tipped pass and scored his second touchdown of the game with two seconds left. That gave Tampa Bay nine defensive touchdowns for the season, meeting the lofty goal Gruden had set. More importantly, though, the Bucs ended the season with the Lombardi Trophy as Super Bowl champions.

Defensive tackle Warren Sapp kisses the Lombardi Trophy after the Bucs won Super Bowl XXXVII to claim their first championship.

Quarterback Brad Johnson lost all four games he started for the Buccaneers in 2004.

CHAPTER 5

NEW BEGINNINGS

The Buccaneers had to give up a lot in the trade to acquire Jon Gruden. Few were complaining after Gruden led the Bucs to a Super Bowl title in his first season. And with Gruden in charge of a talented roster, Tampa Bay looked as if it could remain competitive for years.

However, trading so many high draft picks began to take its toll. While Tampa Bay's core remained mostly intact from 2002 to 2003, several of the defensive stars were older than 30. After a disappointing 7–9 season in 2003, veterans John Lynch and Warren Sapp left in free agency. The Bucs faltered even more in 2004 and finished 5–11.

The Buccaneers stuck with Gruden through the down years. Team officials knew he was in a tough situation but believed in his ability to find success again. Their patience paid off when Gruden led the Bucs to division titles in 2005 and 2007. However, the team lost at home in the opening round both times.

In 2008, the Bucs started the season 9–3 and looked to be on their way to another playoff appearance. Instead, they lost their final four games, including a home loss to the Oakland Raiders in the season finale to miss the postseason. By then, the team's patience had run out. Following the late-season collapse, the Bucs fired Gruden. Even though the team ultimately declined in Gruden's later years, many in Tampa defended the original trade. That included former Tampa Bay defensive back Dwight Smith. He said, "This is what people don't understand: One Super Bowl is worth 20 years of mediocrity."

Buccaneers head coach Jon Gruden became known for his fiery attitude during games.

"THIS IS WHAT PEOPLE DON'T UNDERSTAND: ONE SUPER BOWL IS WORTH 20 YEARS OF MEDIOCRITY."

—DWIGHT SMITH

Raheem Morris joined Tampa Bay's coaching staff in 2002.

LONG DROUGHT

Gruden was 39 when he lifted the Bucs to a championship, making him the youngest head coach to win a Super Bowl at the time. When the team looked for a coach to replace him, it opted for someone even younger. The Bucs promoted their 32-year-old defensive coordinator, Raheem Morris, to head coach.

After a 3–13 debut in 2009, Morris led the Bucs to a 10–6 record in his second season. But that record was only good enough to finish third in their division, and the Bucs missed out on the playoffs. That ended up being the only time Tampa Bay came close to the postseason for years. The team fired Morris after a 4–12 record in 2011 and began cycling through coaches and quarterbacks.

The low point came in 2014, when Tampa Bay finished with a league-worst record of 2–14. That at least gave Bucs fans some hope, as the team received the top pick in the 2015 draft. Quarterback Jameis Winston was the obvious choice. He had recently won the 2013 Heisman Trophy and led Florida State to a national championship.

The strong-armed Winston showed promise early in his career and made the Pro Bowl as a rookie. But his frequent turnovers made it difficult for the Bucs to escape mediocrity. No season showed off the hot-and-cold nature of Winston more than 2019. That year, Winston threw 33 touchdowns and led the NFL with 5,109 passing yards. He also threw a league-high 30 interceptions. It marked the first time a quarterback had ever thrown 30 touchdowns and 30 interceptions in the same season.

Tampa Bay had hired head coach Bruce Arians ahead of the 2019 season. After one year of watching Winston, he was fed up with the quarterback's constant turnovers. With Winston's contract up after the 2019 season, the Bucs set out to find a new quarterback to lead the team.

Quarterback Jameis Winston threw for more than 4,000 yards in three different seasons with the Bucs.

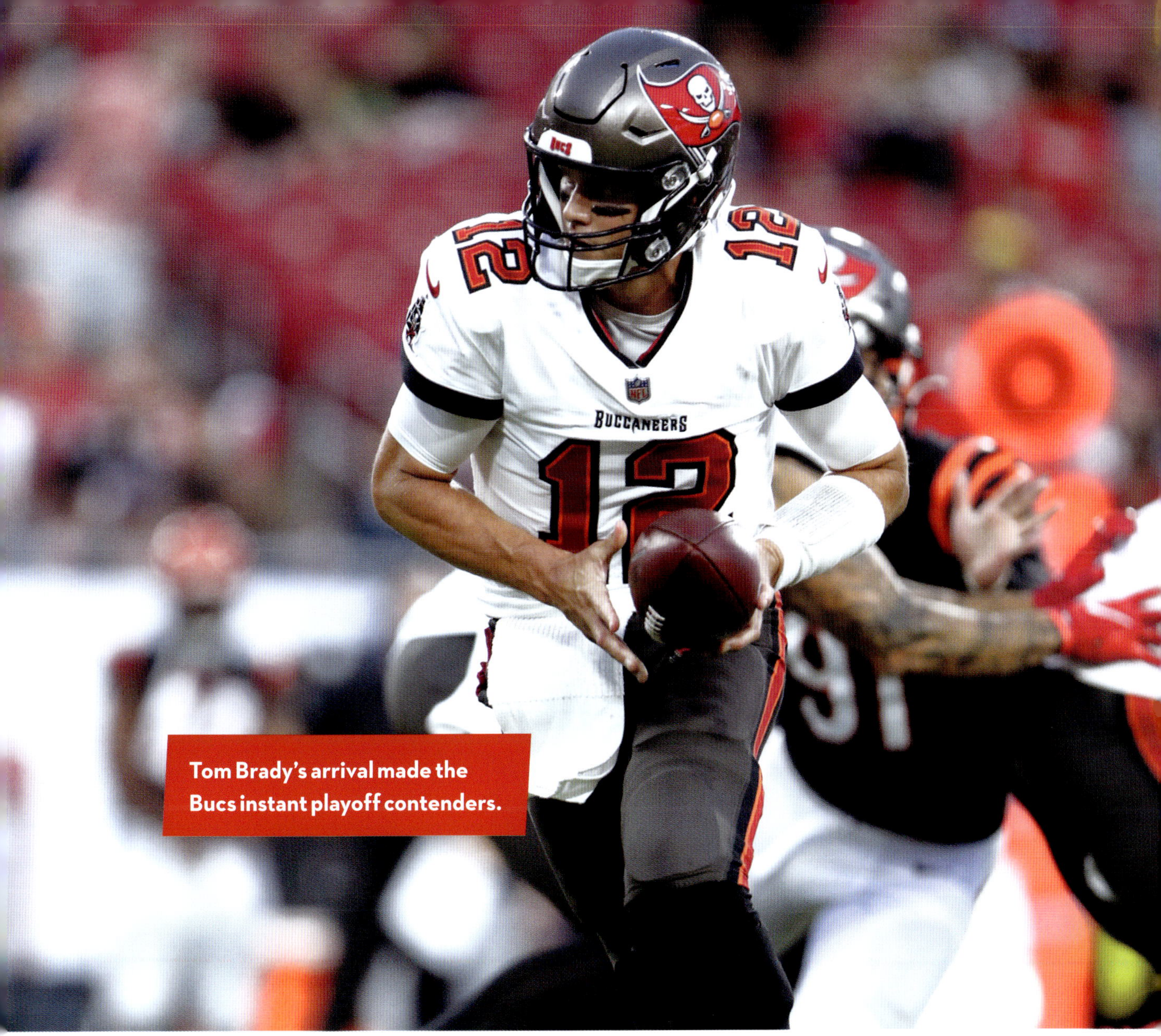
Tom Brady's arrival made the Bucs instant playoff contenders.

GETTING THE G.O.A.T.

Though the Bucs had enjoyed some success in the 2000s and won a Super Bowl, Tampa Bay was hardly one of the NFL's glamour teams. But when opportunity presented itself in 2020, the Bucs went for it. Tom Brady, the NFL's most successful quarterback ever, was looking for a new team. Many teams wanted to show the superstar that they gave him the best opportunity to win a Super Bowl. In the end, he picked Tampa Bay.

In some ways, it was an odd choice, given the Bucs' lack of recent playoff success. But Brady saw a roster with talented wide receivers such as Mike Evans and Chris Godwin. And the Bucs saw a quarterback who, despite being 43 years old, could bring a winning mentality to the young team.

Mike Evans recorded more than 1,000 receiving yards in each of his first 11 seasons with the Bucs.

After 20 seasons and six Super Bowl titles with the New England Patriots, Brady experienced some growing pains with his new team. It took time for him and Arians to get on the same page about what kind of offense the team should run. The low point came in a Week 12 loss to the Kansas City Chiefs that dropped the Bucs to 7–5. When things began to click, however, the Bucs suddenly became unstoppable. The Buccaneers won their final four games to finish 11–5 and earn a spot in the playoffs. Then they won

Bucs defensive end Shaquil Barrett hits Kansas City Chiefs quarterback Patrick Mahomes during Super Bowl LV on February 7, 2021.

three consecutive road playoff games to secure a spot in Super Bowl LV and a rematch with the Chiefs.

Behind star quarterback Patrick Mahomes, the defending champion Chiefs presented a daunting task. But Brady had confidence in his teammates. In the days leading up to the game, he sent them a simple text message each night that read, "We will win."

Brady delivered on that message by throwing three touchdown passes in an MVP performance. Many of his teammates stepped up as well. The Chiefs had one of the league's most dangerous offenses. But the physical Tampa Bay defense forced Mahomes into

BOAT PARTY

The Buccaneers celebrated their Super Bowl LV title with a boat parade. Players floated down the Hillsborough River near downtown Tampa as fans cheered from the banks. The unique celebration almost turned into a disaster. At one point, Bucs quarterback Tom Brady tossed the Vince Lombardi Trophy to a teammate on another boat. Thankfully, the teammate caught the trophy, and the celebration continued.

throwing two interceptions. The high-powered Chiefs offense never reached the end zone. With a dominant 31–9 victory, the Buccaneers were Super Bowl champions again.

MOVING ON

After winning his record-extending seventh Super Bowl, Brady had nothing left to prove. He didn't ride off into the sunset after the 2020 season, though. Brady said he wanted to play until he was 45, so he stuck around in Tampa Bay.

In 2021, Brady led the Bucs to their first division title since 2007. Tampa Bay then crushed the Philadelphia Eagles in the first round of the playoffs, setting up a matchup with the Los Angeles Rams. Trailing 27–3 in the third quarter, the Bucs looked down and out. Then Brady led four straight scoring drives to tie the game with 42 seconds left. The comeback effort fell just short, however. The Rams kicked a field goal as time expired to win 30–27.

Even though the Bucs lost, the epic performance could have been a fitting final game for Brady's career. Brady thought so and announced his retirement in February 2022. However, only 40 days later, he came out of retirement for one final season in the NFL. While Brady led the Bucs to another division title, his career came to an end for good with a 31–14 loss to the Dallas Cowboys in the playoffs.

Brady threw for 329 yards against the Los Angeles Rams in their January 2022 playoff meeting.

BUCCANEERS TROPHY CASE

SUPER BOWL CHAMPIONSHIPS: 2

Super Bowl XXXVII – January 26, 2003
Super Bowl LV – February 7, 2021

CONFERENCE CHAMPIONSHIPS: 2

2002, 2020

DIVISION TITLES: 10

NFC Central: 1979, 1981, 1999
NFC South: 2002, 2005, 2007, 2021, 2022, 2023, 2024

All stats are through the 2024 season.

Finding a replacement for the greatest quarterback in NFL history was never going to be easy. Few had high hopes when the replacement turned out to be Baker Mayfield. Though Mayfield had been the top pick in the 2018 draft, his career became derailed by injuries. The Bucs were his fourth team in just six NFL seasons.

Mayfield proved those doubters wrong. With an elite receiver in Evans to throw to, Mayfield lifted the Bucs to a third straight division crown in 2023. Then he torched the Eagles in the playoffs for 337 yards and three touchdowns in a 32–9 wild-card win.

Mayfield and the Bucs kept on winning in 2024. They recovered from a four-game losing streak in the middle of the season to finish 10–7 and claim another NFC South title. Along the way, Mayfield threw a career-high 41 touchdown passes. Evans caught 11 of them. He also surpassed 1,000 receiving yards for the 11th straight year, tying a record set by the legendary Jerry Rice. Although Tampa Bay fell in its first playoff game, Mayfield and the Bucs showed they could still compete among the NFL's very best.

Quarterback Baker Mayfield surpassed 4,000 passing yards and 28 touchdowns in each of his first two seasons in Tampa Bay.

TIMELINE

1976
In Tampa Bay's first NFL season, the Buccaneers go 0–14.

After a 26-game losing streak, the Buccaneers beat the New Orleans Saints for their first NFL win.
1977

The Buccaneers win their division and beat the Philadelphia Eagles to earn their first playoff win.
1979

Following a 6–10 season, John McKay resigns as Tampa Bay's head coach.
1984

1997
In Tony Dungy's second season as coach, the Bucs win their first playoff game since 1979.

1999
Behind a strong defense, the Bucs go 11–5 and eventually reach the NFC Championship Game.

Jon Gruden ends his first season as Bucs head coach by leading the team to its first Super Bowl title on January 26.
2003

The Buccaneers draft Jameis Winston with the top pick in the draft.

2015

Quarterback Baker Mayfield leads Tampa Bay to a fourth straight division title.

2024

2008

After a four-game losing streak to end the season, the Bucs fire Gruden.

2021

Tom Brady lifts the Bucs to their second Super Bowl title on February 7.

2023

Brady retires in February after leading the Bucs to a division title.

GLOSSARY

CEO–short for chief executive officer, the person who is in charge of an organization.

contract–an agreement to play for a certain team.

coordinator–an assistant coach who is in charge of the offense, defense, or special teams.

debut–first appearance.

draft–a system that allows teams to acquire new players coming into a league.

dynamic–energetic and exciting; in sports, usually referring to an athlete with one or more outstanding skills.

expansion team–a new team that is added to an existing league.

free agent–a player who is not signed to a team.

interception–a pass that is caught by a defensive player.

pandemic–a widespread occurrence of an infectious disease.

pick six–an interception returned for a touchdown.

players' strike–a work stoppage due to a disagreement between players and their employers (teams) about things such as working conditions or wages.

Pro Bowl–a postseason competition that the NFL's all-stars are invited to compete in.

retire–to end one's career.

rookie–a professional athlete in his or her first year of competition.

roster–a list of players who make up a team.

sack–a tackle of the quarterback behind the line of scrimmage before he can pass the ball.

scheme–a set of formations that a team regularly uses.

turnover–loss of the ball to the other team through an interception or fumble.

underdog–the person or team that is not expected to win.

veteran–someone who has played for many years.

wild-card–the first round of the playoffs.

ONLINE RESOURCES

To learn more about the Tampa Bay Buccaneers, please visit **abdobooklinks.com** or scan this QR code. These links are routinely monitored and updated to provide the most current information available.